Among the most tumultuous decades in U.S. history, the 1960s were marked by the struggle against racism and poverty, the civil rights revolution, the flowering of the women's movement, the emergence of a "youth culture," and a devastating war in Vietnam. Launched in youthful idealism, many of the reform movements of the sixties sputtered out in violence and cynicism.

The decade began with the election of America's youngest president, John F. Kennedy, who along with his wife, Jackie, personified the glamour and vitality of the "New Frontier." The Kennedy administration was tested by the Berlin Wall, the Bay of Pigs, and the Cuban missile crisis. At home, the unfulfilled promise of the elimination of racial discrimination led to a wave of sit-ins, freedom rides, and desegregation efforts in schools, on buses, in the workplace, and at the lunch counter. Cities such as Selma, Birmingham, and Montgomery, and individuals such as Martin Luther King Jr., Medgar Evers, James Meredith, and Rosa Parks became household names. But by the end of the decade, peaceful civil rights demonstrations had given way to urban riots from Watts to Newark, with rising bitterness exemplified in Malcolm X, Stokely Carmichael, and the Weathermen.

The 1960s witnessed Lyndon Johnson's Great Society, the War on Poverty, Medicare, Project Head Start, the abolishment of the poll tax and literacy tests for voting, the availability of the birth control pill, and America's involvement in the longest and most unpopular foreign war in its history, leading to massive demonstrations and a radically disaffected citizenry.

The decade also saw the development of a "counterculture" vehemently opposed to traditional American ways. Disillusioned young people discovered a society of racism, sexism, imperialism, and oppression. The music of the '60s, from Marvin Gaye to Bob Dylan, was an inseparable part of the turbulent times. In the last year of the decade, Americans saw the culmination of JFK's dream: two American astronauts triumphantly planted human footprints on the moon.

Many of these moments are documented by the Magnum photographers whose work is reproduced in this book of postcards.

the **sixties**
photographs from **Magnum Photos**

Harlem, New York City, 1963
© Leonard Freed/Magnum Photos

BOX 6099 ROHNERT PARK CA 94927

Pomegranate

the **sixties**
photographs from **Magnum Photos**

Coney Island, New York City, 1965
© Danny Lyon/Magnum Photos

BOX 6099   ROHNERT PARK   CA 94927

Pomegranate

HG HERITAGE GRAPHICS INTERNATIONAL MAGNUM PHOTOS

the **sixties**
photographs from **Magnum Photos**

Family portrait, 1962
© Elliott Erwitt/Magnum Photos

CA 94927

ROHNERT PARK

BOX 6099

Pomegranate

the **sixties**
photographs from **Magnum Photos**

Selma March, Alabama, 1965
© Bruce Davidson/Magnum Photos

Pomegranate   BOX 6099   ROHNERT PARK   CA 94927

the **sixties**
photographs from **Magnum Photos**

A health club in Encino, California, 1968
© Dennis Stock/Magnum Photos

BOX 6099 ROHNERT PARK CA 94927

Pomegranate

the sixties
photographs from **Magnum Photos**

Kissing with the flag, 1968
© Roger Malloch/Magnum Photos

BOX 6099   ROHNERT PARK   CA 94927

Pomegranate

the sixties

photographs from **Magnum Photos**

Bank, New York City, 1960
© Henri Cartier-Bresson/Magnum Photos

BOX 6099 ROHNERT PARK CA 94927

Pomegranate

the sixties
photographs from **Magnum Photos**

Folk music near Cornell University, 1964
© Cornell Capa/Magnum Photos

Pomegranate   BOX 6099   ROHNERT PARK   CA 94927

the **sixties**
photographs from **Magnum Photos**

Civil rights protest, 1962
© Bruce Davidson/Magnum Photos

Pomegranate

BOX 6099   ROHNERT PARK   CA 94927

the **sixties**
photographs from **Magnum Photos**

Lincoln Park, Chicago, 1968
© Roger Malloch/Magnum Photos

Pomegranate BOX 6099 ROHNERT PARK CA 94927

the sixties
photographs from **Magnum Photos**

Flower power, 1968
© Dennis Stock/Magnum Photos

BOX 6099   ROHNERT PARK   CA 94927

Pomegranate

the **sixties**
photographs from **Magnum Photos**

**Freedom Day demonstration, Selma,
Alabama, 1964**
© Danny Lyon/Magnum Photos

BOX 6099   ROHNERT PARK   CA 94927

Pomegranate

the **sixties**
photographs from **Magnum Photos**

Amagansett Beach, Long Island,
New York, 1969
© Elliott Erwitt/Magnum Photos

Pomegranate   BOX 6099   ROHNERT PARK   CA 94927

the **sixties**
photographs from **Magnum Photos**

Surfer, 1968
© Dennis Stock/Magnum Photos

BOX 6099   ROHNERT PARK   CA 94927

the **sixties**
photographs from **Magnum Photos**

Sharecroppers, South Carolina, 1965
© Costa Manos/Magnum Photos

Pomegranate

BOX 6099   ROHNERT PARK   CA 94927

the sixties
photographs from **Magnum Photos**

Towing a skateboarder, 1967
© Leonard Freed/Magnum Photos

BOX 6099   ROHNERT PARK   CA 94927

Pomegranate

the **sixties**
photographs from **Magnum Photos**

Selma march, Alabama, 1963
© Bob Adelman/Magnum Photos

Pomegranate   BOX 6099   ROHNERT PARK   CA 94927

the **sixties**
photographs from **Magnum Photos**

Couple at a Vietnam War protest, 1968
© Roger Malloch/Magnum Photos

Pomegranate   BOX 6099   ROHNERT PARK   CA 94927

the **sixties**
photographs from **Magnum Photos**

Hair salon, 1965
© Costa Manos/Magnum Photos

BOX 6099   ROHNERT PARK   CA 94927

Pomegranate

 HERITAGE GRAPHICS INTERNATIONAL

 MAGNUM PHOTOS

the sixties
photographs from **Magnum Photos**

SNCC sit-in, Atlanta, Georgia, 1963
© Danny Lyon/Magnum Photos

BOX 6099   ROHNERT PARK   CA 94927

Pomegranate

the **sixties**
photographs from **Magnum Photos**

March on the Pentagon, 1967
© Leonard Freed/Magnum Photos

BOX 6099   ROHNERT PARK   CA 94927

Pomegranate

HERITAGE GRAPHICS INTERNATIONAL

the **sixties**
photographs from **Magnum Photos**

Demonstration, 1960s
© Danny Lyon/Magnum Photos

Pomegranate

BOX 6099   ROHNERT PARK   CA 94927

HG HERITAGE GRAPHICS INTERNATIONAL

MAGNUM PHOTOS

the sixties
photographs from **Magnum Photos**

Computer room, 1969
© Costa Manos/Magnum Photos

BOX 6099 ROHNERT PARK CA 94927

Pomegranate

the sixties
photographs from Magnum Photos

**Intersection of Grand and Division,
Chicago, 1965**
© Danny Lyon/Magnum Photos

BOX 6099 ROHNERT PARK CA 94927

Pomegranate

the **sixties**
photographs from **Magnum Photos**

Miss North Carolina pageant, 1961
© Burt Glinn/Magnum Photos

BOX 6099   ROHNERT PARK   CA 94927

Pomegranate

the **sixties**

photographs from **Magnum Photos**

Running for sheriff of Greene County, Alabama, 1966. Many constituents will vote for the first time in the election.

© Wayne Miller/Magnum Photos

BOX 6099   ROHNERT PARK   CA 94927

Pomegranate

HERITAGE GRAPHICS INTERNATIONAL

MAGNUM PHOTOS

the **sixties**
photographs from **Magnum Photos**

March on Washington, 1963
© Bruce Davidson/Magnum Photos

BOX 6099   ROHNERT PARK   CA 94927

Pomegranate

the **sixties**
photographs from **Magnum Photos**

Vietnam War protest, 1969
© Roger Malloch/Magnum Photos

Pomegranate

BOX 6099   ROHNERT PARK   CA 94927

the sixties

photographs from **Magnum Photos**

Freedom riders, Montgomery, Alabama, 1961

© Bruce Davidson/Magnum Photos

Pomegranate

BOX 6099   ROHNERT PARK   CA 94927

HERITAGE GRAPHICS INTERNATIONAL

MAGNUM PHOTOS

the sixties
photographs from **Magnum Photos**

Body painting, 1968
© Dennis Stock/Magnum Photos

BOX 6099 ROHNERT PARK CA 94927

Pomegranate